Patricia,
   This is for you, an ~~...~~ a Powerful woman that shines so brightly in the world. Our devine appointment, is simply one of the myriad gifts, opportunities, & miracles that have been placed before us to experience. May this book add an incredible amount of inspiraetion to you & to all of the Lives that you are in contact with. To Love peace, power, & Joy... May you always be connected & Swimming in the Goodness.

SWIMMING
IN THE
GOODNESS

THE GOLDEN GUIDE

HELPING MILLIONS OF PEOPLE LIVE
AMAZING AND EXTRAORDINARY LIVES

Swimming in the Goodness, The Golden Guide

Kirkeby, Aaron Christopher

      Swimming in the Goodness

      ISBN 978-0-692-54311-5

Book Design by Aaron Christopher Kirkeby

This publication has been created to provide a process on a subject for cultivating success. It is sold with the understanding that neither Aaron Christopher Kirkeby nor the Publisher are held responsible where technical or personal knowledge is required. Any legal, physical, mental, financial, spiritual, emotional, social, or personal knowledge or expertise should be acquired by consulting individuals, companies, or organizations in their respective fields that best offer such information or professional advice/services.

Published by Kirkeby Industries LLC

Manufactured in the United States of America. Copies are printed in either Charleston, SC; Middletown, DE; or San Bernardino, CA.

Bulk Purchasing

Please contact Aaron Christopher Kirkeby at info@swimminginthegoodness.com

ACKNOWLEDGEMENT

Special thanks to Greg Reid, your time is very much appreciated. Kurt Doldinger, Khushna Shah, Greg Gagnon, Kellie Legare, Jeff Salz, Lisa Jaffe, Khriste Close and the rest of you who are "Swimming in It" with me, thank you for your guidance, support, and love.

To my two beautiful daughters Athena and Danielle, I love you. This book, <u>Swimming in the Goodness</u>, will help each of you to live amazing and extraordinary lives. The both of you already know that so many dreams have already come and gone. Know yourselves inside and out, and love yourselves. Have self-worth, self-value, self-esteem, love others, and know that you can do anything that you put your mind to. God and the universe is there to conspire with you and help your dreams come true, just believe and have faith.

To all of my friends and family who support me, thank you and I love you. To all of you reading this book, many blessings to you and I love you too. Enjoy this book! Live it and please know that it is a deep pleasure of mine that we have crossed paths.

CONTENTS

INTRODUCTION

This book has been inspired by a dream which had awaken me during the wee hours of the morning in January of 2011. There was a dynamic energy flowing through. A creative inspiration directing the basic script and outline. With this knowing, it is an honor of mine to have been so fortunate with this vision and the ability to write this book. The intention of this book is *to help millions of people live amazing and extraordinary lives*. People like yourself. Lives that are worth abundant and rich blessings. Lives that are given goodness and joys that are truly inspirational. It all stems from having a guide. A point of focus that requires joy and discipline to live a life of passion and purpose.

It is important at this time that I am clear with you. The fact is that by July 2015, so many of the goals I had listed in January 2011 have already come into fruition. Yes! I write to you with the confidence and knowing that I am currently living many of my dreams that I had written four years earlier. This book can help any person step into their dreams.

We all have dreams, wants, and desires that rest inside of us awaiting to come to see the light of day. These desires that compel you and motivate you to continue forward have purpose, they cannot be disregarded. The rejecting of our dreams leads to futility, depression, sadness, and misery. The experiencing of our dreams allows contentment, joy, attractiveness, and thriving lives that impact the world around. This book is currently changing the lives of many people who are already on course. It is a positive influential force in their lives that is creating amazing results.

Thank you for your interest in this book! For knowing that you are worth an amazing existence. For applying yourself to the Goodness. For writing down your dreams. And most of all, for the willingness to see your dreams culminate.

Swimming in the Goodness

"Swimming in the Goodness, the Golden Guide" is a simple system that only has to be followed. You are the captain of your vessel. Remember, life happens. There is a whole ocean out there. Sometimes the ocean is calm and other times the ocean is brutal. As long as you stay in your vessel and mind your own ship, you stay afloat. Let any of that outside negativity in and you can sink. So do not mind the negative people and even the calm people. Mind your own business, stay on course. Sustain and maintain your vessel and you my friend, will always be "Swimming in the Goodness".

Honor your inner truths, your inner workings, your dreams, and your genuine purpose here on earth. Be awed by the light that resides within you. There is a dynamic power that you are connected with. Live in the fruits of the spirit. Blossom by your beautiful truth and experience. Share those fruits and this book with others. Lastly, see others flourish and multiply.

"Swimming in the Goodness" should bring a smile to your face and even make you chuckle. It is a term that I frequently use in response to a person when they ask me how am I doing. It basically means inner joy and inner happiness regardless of any circumstance or environment. All of the space around us is Goodness. The air, the tangible things in life - the walls, cars, and chairs that surround us are all made up of "Goodness" and we all are "Swimming in it." There is not any area around us that is not filled with the Goodness. At any time that we so decide, we have the power to change our circumstances and our environments. In any moment we can live in the "Goodness" of our heart's truest desires.

This book is composed into 3 sections. The first part provides information on the process and how it works. This section provides helpful information in thinking about your goals and explains timing. The second section is where you write down your goals and dreams. This section is what we resort to daily or weekly that gives us our tasks to be completed for the week or day. We check off the steps or dreams that have been accomplished and keep moving forward. The third section provides extra information to help refine our dreams, goals, and ambitions. This section we write down our goals accomplished. And also where we create new ambitions to further expand and grow.

Swimming in the Goodness

It is since 2006 that I have come to begin a deeper understanding and purpose of life. Rebuilding a life that is truly amazing and extraordinary. Having started Swimming in the Goodness and applying the Golden Guide Principles in January of 2011, it is in the course of the last 4 years that I have really begun to escalate to new found heights of accomplishment. Which is why it is now time to share this principles of Goodness with you. From 2011 to 2015 I had gone from a man who did not own a home to a man that owns a 4 bedroom home with a rental property. From being a man without a college degree to a man who earned a Business Degree with a concentration in Organizational Management. Yes, I guess you can say that I was on the twenty-year college program. Sidetracked needless to say. Went from being an every other weekend father to raising my daughters full time. Became less unhappy and discontented to feeling happy and purposeful. By becoming more generative, contributive, and action oriented, my environment and circumstances changed for the better. Definitely Swimming in the Goodness nowadays, which is what I share with others. I mentor and coach many people and this is the culmination of that work.

With proven success, there is no greater joy than to see others having an amazing and extraordinary experience. It is your time now! Share this with others and be a part of their Goodness. This is an invitation to you to become a part of The Swimming in the Goodness family. We create our successes together, share these successes, build momentum, and help others to do the same. This book is the catalyst from living an average life to an amazing life. It is an honor of mine to be a part of this with you.

CHAPTER 1

SEVEN AREA'S FOR GOAL SETTING

There are seven fundamental area's that comprise a person's life. When we think of life, we often hear people speak of their body, soul, and mind. We hear of people talk about being involved in sports and other social activities. People discuss monetary investments, building stronger character, and talk about where they are going on their family's next vacation. With such an array of vast discussions and topics, there seems to be so much out there, to do and experience. The function of Swimming in the Goodness, the Golden Guide is to help people like yourself achieve living lives that are amazing and extraordinary. We will focus our attention on seven main aspects of living where we can set goals. The seven aspects of being are: Physical, Mental, Financial, Spiritual, Emotional, Social, and Personal.

These seven aspects that compose a person's life are the governing factors that shape the lives that we live. The most important thing that any person can do is to be mindful and conscious of what it is they are doing, in each aspect of their life. For instance, a person may have their physical aspect of being as a priority in comparison to the other six areas of their life. Becoming more lean and fit may be their focus, so knowing what to eat and how to eat would be important. Knowing when to exercise and how to exercise are also critical in achieving a physical goal. Correct? Absolutely! Every person that takes action and makes a beginning will have rewarding results in their endeavor if they remain consistent.

The objective of Swimming in the Goodness is to create experiences that provide us with internal rewards. The key to success is applying yourself and committing to Swimming in the Goodness and the principles of this Golden Guide. By committing to these principles you'll be more successful in attaining your goals, no matter how difficult the goals may be. This Golden Guide will ensure that you progress. Making real results in things unreal, like your dreams. Things in which you cannot yet feel or see in your current environment or circumstance. It is only felt and seen when closing your eyes and dreaming.

So by all means, be a dreamer! More importantly, use this book as your vehicle that transforms your dreams into reality. Become an example of success not only for your soul's satisfaction but to be a demonstration for others to follow. Success builds success. Show them how you did it and allow the Golden Guide to impact their lives as well. By helping others, you can only enrich your own experience.

In each of the seven areas, the more specific that we define our goals the easier it will be to complete our goals. Once the goal has been completed, we commence to write new goals and follow the same course of action. It's in the application of this simple system that we are able to live amazing and extraordinary lives. At this time, let us look at the seven areas of our concern.

Physical Goals

Physical goals can come in any array of dreams or desires. What matters here is what you are feeling and what you are wanting to experience in life. Physical natures include things that benefit our health and well-being. Our movement, the things that we do, the way we look, and the way we show up in the world. Being free of disease, being healthy and powerful. Having healing take place, having alignment and physical comfort restored. These are vital aspects within the physical realm of setting goals. The truth is that most happy and successful people workout daily for 30 minutes and have healthy diets. Which means eating organic, non-processed foods.

What you choose to write down as your physical goals will depend on your current physical condition. If you are healthy, you may want to incorporate new goals and new experiences to sustain your current level of good health. If you are currently in a poor state of physical health, it is crucial that you write down goals that will contribute towards good health. For example, exercising thirty minutes every day, reducing the amount of "fast food" that you eat, and eliminating caffeinated drinks.

For instance, if you are overweight, you may have a goal to be healthy. Well what does that mean? It would be a suggestion of mine to not be concerned about weight as much as what you are putting into your body. You may have a goal to weigh 135 pounds but perhaps that weight would be detrimental to your health. Compared to a weight of 148 pounds.

If you had a disease, like cancer, then you would have to make some drastic changes in your life to beat it. A healthy alkaline diet and exercise would be a great preventative measure. Whatever your scenario may be, follow your internal guide, your inner voice. Your inner voice is directing you towards your purpose. Listening to this inner voice is something that would benefit you profoundly. It may direct you to a particular diet, doctor, or a type of exercise that will benefit you and your lifestyle. The purpose of being, is to thrive. To live in joy, happiness, and connection.

Some Physical Goals examples include the following (Please consult your doctor prior to exercising to ensure the training will promote your physical health):

Exercise: Weight lifting, yoga, cross-fit training, competing in triathlons, running, rock climbing, signing up for an obstacle race like The Spartan Race, Tai Chi or Chi Gong, resistance training, dancing, surfing, and walking or hiking. These are some of the many examples that one can feel impressing upon them to experience.

Diet: Eating whole foods, juicing veggies or fruits, eating right-sized portions, drinking water (mostly), eliminating all sugars, becoming soda free, drinking herbal teas, eating every 3 hours, eating balanced meals at each sitting (*protein* like fish or bison, *carbs* like brown rice, *veggies, and fruit*), minimizing breads, eliminating specific oils, minimizing coffee, taking vitamins, and taking supplements. These are a myriad of things that one might feel compelled to incorporate in their lives.

Well Being: Annual check-ups with physicians or care providers, sleeping 7 to 8 hours a night, massages, personal trainer, naps, acupuncture, dressing nicely (for a well-being spiritual pick me up), a healthy sex life, and meditation. Any of these ideas may be part of your physical pursuits.

The purpose depends on your dreams and goals. Be mindful that physical exercise goals incorporate the following; endurance, strength, balance, and flexibility. How is it that you would like to see yourself in 5 years? And if you don't know then who does? That is not a fruitful thought. Our aim is to know exactly how we want to be, what we would like to experience, and that we are worth it. We are here to pursue our dreams! By taking viable action and applying ourselves to our dreams, we achieve our goals. This is the path of living amazing and extraordinary lives.

It is important to be specific and clear with yourself as best you can. The clearer the vision or dream, the easier it will be to manifest and live.

Mental Goals

Defining Mental Goals is an important part of becoming successful and living the life of your dreams. We all have goals that challenge us mentally. There are experiences that we want to live and knowing what these are is important. Naturally, some people may have strengths or weaknesses in any of the seven areas of goal setting. By knowing our strengths and weaknesses, we are able to grow and become more successful.

Some Mental Goal examples include the following:

Educational: Educational pursuits like earning a Master's Degree, a doctorate, or a diploma. Joining a trade to become an electrician, auto tech, machining, or general contractor.

Learning: Performing Arts like acting, dancing, music like piano, drums, or guitar, song writing, ballet, opera, or even a martial art. Visual Arts or Fine arts like painting or drawing, crafts, ceramics, photography, graphic design, film-making, fashion design, sculpting, poetry, or interior design. The Sciences like physics, mathematics, biology, chemistry, or oceanography. The Behavioral and Social

Sciences like psychology, sociology, economics, or political science. Learning business, finances, or entrepreneurship. Learning computers, programs, or games.

General: Reading more books, improving mindset, thinking positive, becoming a more confident speaker, strengthening memory skills, reading faster, comprehending better, inventing, or visioning desired outcomes.

Your motivation towards your individual goals depends solely on what resonates within you. The things that we care about and wish to see come to life is what we should focus our energies on. Just be clear and concise, and you will achieve each dream one at a time.

Financial Goals

Financial goals are important as everyone is well aware. If you have nothing to aim towards, you can see how ineffective your energy is being directed. Having set financial dreams and clear aspirations will motivate you to get out of bed each morning. This depends on your current belief of money, how you desire to use money, and how money will benefit you and those around you.

There is only one difference between a person who is wealthy in comparison to a person who is in debt. The person who is affluent has better defined goals and can see their works manifested. You have to see it first in order to achieve it. That is true in any area of our lives. So be as clear as you can be, in regards to your aspirations and goals. If you think poorly of yourself, then you will live poorly. If you think abundantly of yourself, then you will live an abundant and rich life. Remember, **you are the captain of your vessel, nobody else is.** Nobody controls your financial aspect of being. If someone does, then I strongly suggest that your first goal that you write down is to become financially independent from that person.

Some Financial Goals examples include the following:

Investments: Invest in a start-up company, stocks, bonds, or mutual funds. Start a company of your own using your own resources. Real estate investments to flip or rent. Direct marketing. Loaning your money for a friends business endeavor can be a great way to invest your resources. Investing in your own personal growth is another possible goal you may have. Investing money is the best thing that a person can do with their allocated resources.

Savings: You may have goals in sight for building a healthy savings. Having cash available and ready to use in emergency situations. Savings for your long and short term goals is smart to consider.

Spending: Knowing how much you would like to spend. Being responsible with resources. Budgeting where resources will be going. These are great ways to build success.

Giving: Donate a portion of resources to various organizations that feed your soul, like a church or a non-profit organization. Philanthropic or tithing goals are great to establish. These are great ways to contribute back into our community. This also offers a sense of belonging and self-worth.

Worth: Knowing how much you would like to be worth. Knowing how much you would like to have in your savings account, investments, and cash on hand. How much money you would like to earn this year. Knowing if you would like to own your own company. Having clear career goals. Defining your financial paths are critical while scripting your amazing and extraordinary life.

By understanding each aspect of financial goal setting, growth is promoted. We become guided into directions previously unfathomable. If there is something pressing on your consciousness to build, just begin or start it, take the first step. No matter how absurd it may appear or how difficult it may seem, each goal can be achieved if we persist. Once you have accomplished everything you had written, the next step will surely present itself to you in order to progress. All we have to do is work, take initiative, and take the next indicated step. If you don't, that dream that was perfectly placed within you will not materialize. You are your dreams outlet!

Trust your instincts and follow your heart. No one else can live out your dreams for you and even if they did, how would that benefit you? Arise from that darkness of the unknown and of fear. Live from the power and knowing that resides within your inner guidance. The Golden Guide is the method that will allow you to make sense of these various aspects of being. This guide will separate you from the old behaviors that provided minimal results, while developing new behaviors that propel you to higher ground and offer you more clarity, more understanding, and more worth.

Spiritual Goals

Spiritual Goals are a valuable aspect of men and women. Many people who have accomplished extraordinary tasks were content in the fact that we are part of something much bigger than ourselves. That our being here, has purpose. That we can come to understand certain principles and come to see results that regardless of a person's belief establishes faith that certain habits provide certain results. For everything is cause and effect. So within, so without. This is ancient wisdom indeed.

If at this particular time you may not have the inclination to define any spiritual goals, I would like to ask you to at least venture here and attempt. If I told you about a tasty restaurant and you never tried it, how can you ever know that it would make your palate dance with joy? Be bold here.

Meditation: Meditative goals can be learning various meditational techniques, breathing exercises, sitting silently, visualizations, periodic soul searching, yoga, Tai Chi or Chi gong.

Prayer: Praying goals can be a great way to grow personal strength and understanding. Establishing prayer partnerships are a great way to ensure that you stay accountable in your spiritual growth. Arranging set times in your daily schedule to get re-grounded and connected by prayer can be a goal of yours. Developing heightened compassion, joy, healing, serenity, purpose, and love are area's you may strive to increase.

Affiliations: Becoming involved in an organized religion may be a personal goal of yours. Trying out various churches or beliefs that promote healthy lifestyles for yourself and others meanwhile respecting other beliefs. Getting involved in organizations or meet-up groups that share similar beliefs or mind-sets as your own. Volunteering on a trip to carry the word of your faith and help homeless people. Seeking spiritual counsel and friendships.

Connection: Tithing & philanthropy are ways to contribute financially and is a great way to turn prayer into action. Contributing a small portion of your resources (time, treasure, and/or talent) is a beneficial way to give back to that which feeds and nourishes your soul. Developing your faith, reading spiritual or self-help books are also great avenues to pursue. Traveling to a particular spiritual or religious destination. Retreats and workshops may be some of your spiritual goals. Writing spiritual books is a great way to connect with others.

Whatever your spiritual goals may be, define them clearly, stretch yourself, and be open to a new and better experience. Get involved, take action, and allow your own inner truth to shine so you can impact others in a positive fashion that enables them to shine as well.

Faith is one of those intangible things in life. The only way to develop faith is to incorporate any of these intangible approaches which in time will become tangible and understood by practicing them daily. We all have faith that the sun will rise and be there in the morning so perhaps faith is something that isn't so far-fetched. Perhaps faith is something that is for every man and woman regardless of their religious or non-religious involvement. The whole point of faith is to trust in a higher good and to be connected to that higher good that is found within. This will allow you to be a demonstration of great works being done.

Emotional Goals

Emotional goals are a great way to grow as individuals. Understanding how we operate, what moves us, our strengths and weaknesses, and knowing what type of person we would like to grow into are all vital in developing our character. It is natural for us to change and grow. Being mindful of the type of person we would like to be will catapult us into new experiences and joys.

If we find that we could be happier by losing the tendency of anger or fear, then we have more capacity to grow emotionally. A term that I regularly use in response to how people ask me how I am doing is, "Swimming in the Goodness." Another response may be, "Amazing." The truth is that I am swimming in the Goodness and so can you. It is all around. The amount of joy and happiness that we feel is cultivated and developed. The only question is to ask yourself, "Do I want to be Swimming in the Goodness?" The answer is absolutely! Most certainly you should want to be! Because, if you are, more good and amazing things happen in your life!

This Golden Guide is the path that we get to use to allow this Goodness to multiply and grow. When it comes to our emotional aspect of being and our emotional health, being mindful of how we wish to show up in the world is imperative. Being a magnet, being attractive, and being a person that shines is difficult to ignore.

Areas to consider setting emotional goals include the following:

Support: Having a life coach or a mentor, being involved in an organization, helping others, learning about other people's success, sharing our own success, counseling, retreats, getaways, being a mentor, listening, journaling, having a supportive spouse, developing relationships both personal or business, volunteering, and feeling connected to others.

Stability: Self -Love, self-worth, self-esteem, arranging time for relaxation, massages, calmness, serenity, joy, happiness, compassion, reading self-help books, free from anger, managing how we react to people or situations, feeling connected, personal time, having purpose, balancing our time, being disciplined in actions and behaviors that keep us emotionally intact and grounded, confidence, breathing exercises, addiction free, learning new activities or arts, contributing to others, laughing more, stepping into the unknown confidently, having healing, living life to the fullest, living with passion, and being more vulnerable and open to new experiences, evening walks.

These are all examples of goals that you can adopt in order to grow more emotionally sound. Having emotional support is vital to emotional soundness of mind. As you write down your own emotional goals, it is important to have a clear picture in your mind of the type of person that you would like to become. Who is it that you have seen or known that you truly admire? What are the actions that you would like to mimic? When we admire particular traits of others, it is because we would like to embody those traits.

Social Goals

Social goals are important to define because who we associate with is exactly who we are. If you find yourself around people who are prosperous, chances are you yourself are prosperous. Homeless people tend to hang around other homeless people. It is just the nature of how life is. If you surf, chances are you hang out with other surfers during the week. If you had a particular illness, chances are that you associate with those who encountered the same illness.

The point is "like" attracts "like". If you don't find a group that you like, a group of people will find you. If you are liking what you keep experiencing then you my friend are Swimming in the Goodness! While being on a good path, you may want to refine your goals or create new goals to increase your self-worth and joy. Life is a continuing upward spiral so make the best of it and enjoy it!

If you are unhappy about the circumstance or environment which you encounter daily, then it's time to make changes. Your inner-guide is driving you towards better experiences. Perhaps you have an addiction that is creating unpleasant experiences over and over. It is important to find an organization, a person, or arrange counseling that can help you recover from that life draining peril. Perhaps you have never sought to join a group or organization because of fear. Well it is time to be bold. Add more joy to yourself and to others by sharing your presence with that group. This is your life we are talking about here. Is it boring? Is it fun? Is it hard or challenging? Well good to any of those answers! Why? Because this Golden Guide is going to help you create a life worth talking about to your friends, loved ones, and even with strangers.

Activities/Clubs/Groups: Playing a sport that you have always wanted to do, learning a language, arts and crafts, playing in a band, business networks, book club, dancing, volunteering, business outreach or mentorships, church, philanthropy, a science club, meet-up groups, traveling to another country and volunteering time building a home or helping the sick, starting a group of your liking and helping others find joy in their life, organizing groups, teaching others a gift or trade that you know, public speaking, the list can go on and on.

When it comes to your involvement within your community, what would you like to experience? What would you like to contribute? In life, it is often a direct result that what we put into something is what we get out of it. Therefore, if we put nothing into our community, then nothing changes, it stays the same. If we throw trash on the streets, well we are contributing to making our community look trashy and uncared for. If we pick up trash, if we make a park for children to play, if we add to our community that betters those around, our lives become rich and full. Being wealthy does not only mean with money. There is wealth in any area of or lives. We can be wealthy in friendships, happiness, knowledge, influencing others, and with insight. Being rich in laughter is a beautiful thing!

This book is a guide to allow you to step into that golden side of yourself, where you live your passions every day. From the time that you wake up till the time that you retire for the night can be marvelous. Have passion in your life. Surround yourself with people that bring the best out of you. People that you enjoy being around. Make goals and accomplish those goals. Once those goals have been accomplished, create new goals. Create new goals that move you upward. That allow you to view life fully and wholly.

Personal Goals

Personal goals are those things that reside in our hearts. Personal goals are those hidden dreams that we have put off for so long. On occasion these surface to remind us that they are still within. Who we want to be as a person, whether we want to be happily married or happily single (hey, happily is the key word). Whether we want to travel and see the world. The goals you make define who you are as a person. The novel invention or idea that you have that you know would help out so many people is there for a reason.

Our personal desires are real. There is no denying our deep seated beliefs or genuine wants. It's not like we can play pretend with ourselves. If we feel compelled to live in a beautiful home in the mountains by a lake, why settle for anything less? If we want to see a view of the ocean from our bedroom window, we must set the goal in order to get there. You have to see and feel this desire. It is up to each of us to trust the process that the dream of how we want to live, wake up, and spend our day is one hundred percent real. It is up to us to believe that it can happen. That dream will motivate and set things in action both seen and unseen. Soon enough, you will be living in this dream. This will bring deep inner-satisfaction and joy. Try it and see for yourself. Be bold in your dreams. Step out of the box and explore the possibilities. You are worth it. We are worth living amazing and extraordinary lives!

Dreams/Hobbies/Activities: Helping another person, seeing your children excel in life and attend a great university. Having amazing and strong bonds with your children. Adopting young children and giving them love. Living in a home that was custom built near the ocean, being a beacon of light for many others to find their way to living their own dreams and passions, gardening, spending time on occasion dreaming and visualizing, traveling to Australia, Norway, and Fiji, riding a custom motorcycle, skydiving, spending time reading inspiring books on the beach or near a mountainous lake, owning a successful business that positively impacts others and the community, riding dirt bikes with the family, spending time daily doing several physical activities like yoga, working out, or surfing. Marrying a beautiful person inside and out, having a best friend to experience life with. Gaining new wisdom and sharing it. Owning property. Playing a club sport. Owning a club team. Playing the cello. Family vacations twice a year. Learning stone or wood carving. Having a chef or a cleaning crew. Having an assistant. Having a family. Waking up happy and content every morning and living joyfully every day.

Whatever is in your heart you have to know it, see it, and feel it! What you are doing at this moment is dictating your future. Be hopeful, be positive, and be content knowing that the dreams that we have will happen. Dream and do. It is ancient wisdom, so within, so without. What we see inside of our minds as we dream will certainly be lived in time so think great thoughts. Have a great vision for your life!

There is a golden thread that joins our dreams to us. Trust that no matter how distant that thread may be, the fact that you can see it or feel it, makes it real. See yourself driving the car of your dreams. Marrying the person of your dreams. Living in the home or homes of your dreams. Living a life of passion and going to a place of work to contribute because you love it. Having relationships with the people of your dreams. If you are modest, that is fantastic. Continue to live a life of modesty. Point is to be okay with who you are, with what you want, and what you receive. Love yourself completely. Love yourself remarkably and shine so others can see the joy within themselves.

Completion of Goals

The purpose of goals is for every goal to be achieved and therefore complete. Complete the goals that you set down on paper. This Golden Guide is the method that will enable you to achieve each dream written. See the dreams on paper, achieve each dream, then check it off as complete. Once we complete a goal and enjoy the success of living that dream, we get to write down new goals and dreams. In some circumstances our dreams have to be sustained, so sustain those dreams. Maintaining those dreams have to be our goal.

It is a wonderful fact to know that we all are fortunate enough to dream. It is even more wonderful to know that those thoughts and dreams have the possibility to be lived. Swimming in the Goodness is the way that will allow you to reach the shores of your dreams. This book is the way that will allow you to stand on solid ground. By establishing our own foundation, we inspire others. This practice gives hope. The successful completion of our goals is the proof that we can achieve what we put our minds to. We must stay dedicated to the Golden Guide's design of Swimming in the Goodness.

It is important to note here that in receiving the gifts from achieving a goal, we give credit to where credit is due. It is important to be grateful. It is also important to share the gifts that we have accomplished with others. Tell others about Swimming in the Goodness and how they too can attain their dreams. Be their hope. We tell others about our successes and we encourage others to follow if they so desire. Being an example of triumph, success, and achievement is attractive. It is a wonderful experience indeed to share the joy that we find and help others to "Swim in the Goodness!"

It is also strongly encouraged that you write down your goals in all areas of goal setting. Set goals in the Physical, Mental, Financial, Spiritual, Emotional, Social, and Personal areas. Be thorough, be clear, and be honest with yourself. This is your life we are talking about.

CHAPTER 2

THE ESSENCE OF TIME

This guide of Swimming in the Goodness allows us to use time efficiently in order to create real success over a period of time. It is arranged in such a fashion to enhance accomplishing our goals. While we may set a Financial Goal 5 years from now, we may reach the Financial Goal in 2 years. If that be the case, we would simply move forward the 10 year goal or rewrite a new financial goal.

For the purpose of potency, power, and success, the Timeline Portion has been composed in the following fashion:

10 Year Goals

Long range goals are important to have because they give us a target to aim towards. By setting our sights on long range desires, we have something to strive for. These goals are important when it comes to thinking about where it is that we see ourselves in 10 years. Where do you live, where do you go to work? Are you an owner of an operation or do you have partners in an enterprise? What is it that you would like to be doing for your family and friends? These are all important factors to consider.

In each area of our lives, we define what we dream of experiencing and achieving. It is imperative that we write down our dreams in each of these areas; Physically, Mentally, Financially, Spiritually, Emotionally, Socially, and Personally. Where do you see yourself 10 years from today? These long range goals are a rough prediction and may not be clear but they give us direction. Regardless of how impractical or practical your goals are, anything is possible if you are willing to commit to this process. If you can see yourself doing and feeling an experience, then you can live it. This is truth! Practicality has no place when it comes to dreaming. It is the dreaming that produces practicality and reality. Ask the Wright Brothers. If another person is unable to see your vision, then good. Why would you invest in stock with them by having them encourage your dream which they cannot see? Then be let down because they do not offer you encouragement then you cease taking action on your dreams and it is only you who suffers. It is not them. Remember this always. Trust the dreams that have been placed within you that compels you into action.

It may be your passion to be a professional athlete or a person behind the scenes in a television production. Perhaps you will spend your life gathering data at the North Pole studying the magnetic energy field. What matters is that you can see it, the inner calling and passion that is within you. You may be destined to be an influential person in your local community. As a past time, you may attend hiking adventures in remote mountain ranges with a group of other mountaineers. This is why we have goals, to set our sights. Some of you will be giving lectures in a new area of physics that you discovered. How are we emotionally in 10 years? Are we balanced and disciplined, confident or witty?

It's all up to you! You choose how you want to Swim in the Goodness. Do you own several rental properties? Remember that how we envision ourselves in the future will most likely happen. If we go through the next ten years just being okay, barely getting by, then you will be no better than you were ten years ago. Be alive and hopeful. This is your time to shine and have amazing and extraordinary experiences. Understand that our ten year goals set the standard of what we strive to be today.

5 Year Goals

5 year goals are closer than we think so being clear here is paramount. The best suggestion that I have is for you to understand the following. When we write our ten year goals, how we pursue

these seemingly unreachable goals is by figuring out the half way point. Now those goals that seemed so distant and unattainable begin to be more realistic and reachable.

An example would be a Personal Goal that is set ten years from now. Like seeing yourself living in a beachfront house in the city of Del Mar, California. While in your present situation and circumstances, living in a beachfront house in Del Mar may not be manageable. What would be the half way point at the five year milestone where you could see yourself living comfortably and happily? What are the required tasks to generate the earnings necessary to afford the beach front home in ten years? The answer could be in five years, to own a 4 bedroom home 15 miles away from the beach. This goal of purchasing a home within five years would allow you to get closer to the ten year goal. Building equity in that home during that time, you may decide to keep the home and rent it out while you live in Del Mar ten years from now. The powerful thing to remember is that we are the creators and sculptors of our lives. No other person is. We create the lives that we want to live. Swim in the Goodness!

During the first two years we will have to earn and save the necessary money for the purchase of the home. It is what we get to do to live our dream. This adds motivation to our lives. At year 2 we purchase the home and stay on course. Continuing on with your other goals as you gain momentum and accomplish the goals in the other areas of your life. The fact is that you are able to live an amazing and extraordinary life. A life that has purpose and meaning. A life that is attractive and magnetic.

Some five year goals stand on their own. This means that a goal is not set in the ten year range. It stands on its own accord. For example, you may want to be fluent in Chinese. If this is the case, you can organize the years and months prior accordingly. That way in 5 years from now, all milestones have been completed and you are progressing along in that goal of being fluent in Chinese.

Another example may be in five years, a high school senior wants to be competing professionally in the NFL. If this is your goal, you will be able to set annual milestones preceding the five year mark. Each year raising your performance level in order to accomplish this goal. Set networking goals. Meet players or coaches who will mentor you and guide you to being the best you. A mental goal can be visualizing yourself performing your best in the game. Envision yourself playing for your favorite NFL team.

Writing our 5 year goals is imperative in order to live these experiences. Even more important than that is actually having the dream(s). Having vision is the only thing that separates you from having and not having what you really would like to have. If you lack vision, then you are a poor dreamer and have lost touch with that part of yourself. The things that make you feel happiness in your life can dissipate. If you do not know what you want to do, I highly suggest that you spend time dreaming 10 minutes a day. Think about your past and the things that made you feel genuinely happy as a child or teenager. Things like helping others, playing a sport, or teaching another person how to do mathematics. Whatever it may be, reconnect with your inner joy.

Are you the person that envisions themselves working at a fast food restaurant, or owning one? Are you going on vacations with friends or family and creating memories? Or are you the person not doing these things? Your life is more valuable than watching others go on vacations and having fulfilling experiences, you are worth it too! There is plenty of Goodness for you to swim in! Make a splash and smile, it's what we are here to do.

To sum up five year goals, it is for our benefit to write down in this book what it is we want to experience five years from now. What we see is what will be. If what you see is a bunch of party going, bad ass guys and girls having fun, well guess what? That is exactly who you will follow if you do not write down your own goals and future aspirations. The guys and girls that party, are exchanging 5 years of valuable time that they could have been creating amazing and extraordinary lives. Own your existence. Choose to live with passion, vision, and accomplishment. The only thing that matters is what you decide to do. We are only limited by our own ability to envision what we wish to be. If we can think clearly and see highly of ourselves, we will accomplish towering goals.

1 Year Goals

One year goals are great because these are the goals that are more realistic. Being closer in range, these goals give the long distant goals perspective. This goal setting portion of the book is what really motivates us to stay on course. We will find that many of our yearly goals will be the same for several years in a row in order to accomplish a five year goal.

Some one year goals may be independent of a five year goal. For instance, you may have a goal this year to sky-dive. So list this dream and once it is accomplished, simply check it off and write down a new goal or dream to be lived.

There may be a one year goal that is connected to a five year goal. Perhaps you are pursuing a Masters and Doctorate program at a University of your dreams. While you may be 2 years away from graduating with a Bachelor's degree, your sights are set on completing a doctorate program. Have this five year goal and write down the different steps required to take in each year preceding the five year milestone. So your first year goal would be to complete your 3rd year of undergraduate work. The second year goal would be to apply for the Doctorate Program at the top schools of your choice. Another year two goal would be to graduate with a Bachelor's Degree. Three to five year goals will be to do the Doctorate Program tasks given that are appropriate for that particular year, bringing you closer to achieving that goal.

This is what will keep you on track of your Personal Goal of becoming a Doctor. Have clearly defined goals that are broken down into tasks that are easily taken and managed. We do not stare at the top of the mountain, we simply look up on occasion to glance at the top of the mountain to make sure that we are on course. What we do is look at the next step to take, no matter how tired or how energized we are, we simply keep moving.

Some examples of yearly goals:

Physical goals: Weigh 146 pounds and be healthy, lean and fit. Eat 5 days a week, clean whole meals for breakfast lunch and dinner including snacks. Workout 5 days a week. Have a massage once a month. Hike the Great Himalaya Trail in Nepal.

Mental goals: Completing this year of schooling with a minimum of a 3.7 GPA, learning Spanish, playing on piano Ludwig Van Beethoven's Fur Elise, reading 12 books this year.

Financial Goals: Opening up a small business, employing 6 people, and giving 3% of personal earnings to my favorite non-profit organization.

Spiritual Goals: Volunteering at a hospice organization, Tithing 10% to a church, writing and journaling every night for 5 minutes before going to sleep, meditating and praying throughout the day.

Emotional Goals: Becoming more serene, confident, and choosing to hang around happy people. Developing stronger and healthier habits.

Social Goals: Getting involved and taking on a leadership role in my favorite organization. Dancing with friends often. Volunteer for city fun run. Have a strong business network.

Personal Goals: Take a family vacation to Colorado during the winter and ski. Surf getaway in Costa Rica. Help mentor young adults on living abundant lives. Being a better parent and be more present by listening and spending quality time with your children. Cliff jumping into the ocean.

The goals and dreams that you have are special! No matter how small or how outlandish they may seem, write them down. You can achieve them if you can see and feel them. Your yearly goals are the manageable steps that we take to accomplish those larger goals. We cannot eat a whole loaf of bread. We can enjoy one slice at a time though. Have a vision, write it down, and accomplish your dreams!

6 Month Goals

These closer targeted goals is where we really begin to feel motivated. When we get to the sixth month marker, we are able to see how many tasks have been completed. As well as what next tasks that are required in order to live out our five and ten year goals. We are also able to see what new steps may have to be incorporated to accomplish those goals.

An example here may be that you have a One Year Goal of going on a vacation. So by the sixth month, your goal is to know the costs involved with the trip. The destinations that you would like to see in that city or country, and also attractions or activities that have to be done while on this trip. Zip-Lining, hiking trails, events, restaurants, all should be planned out by the sixth month point. Most importantly, the scheduled date should be known by this time too.

Some examples of 6th Month Goals based from yearly goals would be (*The original year goal will be in italics* and the six month goals will be in regular font):

Physical goals: *Weigh 146 pounds and be healthy, lean, and fit.* Weigh 159 pounds and be healthy, lean and fit at the six month point. Eat 4 days a week clean whole meals for breakfast lunch and dinner including snacks. *Workout 5 days a week.* Workout 4 days a week. Have a massage once a month. *Hike the Great Himalaya Trail, Nepal.* Have the trip planned out by this point. Know who is going on the trip, the dates of the trip, costs involved, the payment due dates for flight, transportation, and stay accommodations.

Mental goals: *Completing this year of schooling with a minimum of a 3.7 GPA.* This semester I will take 3 courses instead of 4, study more by myself or in study groups with classmates, and spend 3 hours a week getting tutored. *Learn Spanish.* Take a Spanish course. *Play on piano Ludwig Van Beethoven's Fur Elise.* Set aside 20 minutes a day for playing piano. *Reading 12 books this year.* Read 6 books

Financial Goals: *Opening up a small business.* Have completed the following for small business; Business plan completed, seek business assistance and training, choose a location for business, financing for business, determine legal structure of business, register business name, get a tax ID number, register for local and state taxes, get business licenses and any permits, and know employer responsibilities. *Employing 6 people.* This goal may be employing 2 people at the six month point, depending on whether or not the establishment is up and running. *Give 3% of personal earnings to my favorite non-profit organization.* This can remain the same, give 3% of personal earnings to my favorite non-profit organization.

Spiritual Goals: *Volunteering at a Hospital.* This can remain the same at the six month mark. *Tithing to my church 10%.* This can remain the same at 6 months. *Writing and journaling every night for 5 minutes before going to sleep.* This can remain the same at 6 months. *Meditating and praying throughout the day.* This can remain the same at 6 months.

Emotional Goals: *Becoming more serene, confident, and hanging around happy people.* This can remain the same at 6 months. *Developing stronger and healthier habits.* This can remain the same at 6 months. Not yelling when angry.

Social Goals: *Getting involved and taking on a leadership role in my favorite organization.* This can remain the same at 6 months. *Dancing with friends often.* This can remain the same at 6 months. *Volunteer for cities Fun Run.* This can remain the same at 6 months. *Have a strong business network.* This can remain the same at 6 months.

Personal Goals: *Take a family vacation to Colorado during the winter and ski. Have chosen the* Hotel, ski resort, or cabin 2 months before Dec. 17. *Surf getaway in Costa Rica.* Get the friend list request written, choose the hotel or house rental and paid for by 2 months out, know of night life hot spots, events, and other must do's. *Help mentor young adults on living abundant lives.* Join an organization that helps youth in the community. *Being a better parent and be more present by listening and spending quality time with children.* Set aside 30 minutes a day for children to connect on a deeper level and to be more present. *Cliff jumping into the ocean.* Find the cliff jumping spots in Costa Rica and any nearby beaches. Also locate any other great cliff jumping beaches and plan a small trip with family and a few friends.

Monthly Goals

Monthly goals makes our 6 months goals even more clear! This is what allows us to stay on course and create effective movement. Movement, action, and application, these things are the key to life. Success requires movement. Swimming in the Goodness Golden Guide is the method that helps us make those movements. It is the key to unlocking the hidden treasures within ourselves.

Our monthly goals are the miniscule details of the painting of our lives. In each goal setting area we simplify the six month goals into 6 individual monthly goals. By breaking down the 6 month goal into monthly goals, we are able to do the next indicated step. Making the next step less difficult. It makes the process more manageable and allows us to execute and attain our dream.

Sentences in italics represent our year goals, normal font is our 6 month goals, and underlines sentences are our monthly goals. This will allow us to see the arrangement branching into smaller more workable steps. Bringing us closer to our dreams and our dreams closer to us.

Physical goals

Weigh 146 pounds and be healthy, lean, and fit. Weigh 159 pounds and be healthy, lean and fit at the six month point. *Workout 5 days a week.* Workout 4 days a week. <u>Weigh 170 pounds by the end of the month. Work out 3 days a week for this first month. Eat clean meals (Breakfast, lunch and dinner including all snacks) 3 days out of the week minimum.</u>

Have a massage once a month. <u>This goal stays the same.</u>

Hike the Great Himalaya Trail, Nepal. Have the trip planned out by this point. Know who is going on the trip, the dates of the trip, costs involved, the payment due dates for flight, transportation, and stay accommodations. <u>Decide date for Nepal hiking trip. Send out invitation to friends asking them to confirm within three weeks if they are interested in going on hiking trip.</u>

Mental goals:

Completing this year of schooling with a minimum of a 3.7 gpa. This semester I will take 3 courses instead of 4, study more by myself and in study groups with classmates, and spend 3 hours a week getting tutored.

Learn Spanish. Take a Spanish course. <u>Register for upcoming Spanish course.</u>

Play on piano Ludwig Van Beethoven's Fur Elise. Set aside a minimum of 20 minutes a day for playing piano. Find a piano teacher and start taking piano lessons by next week to improve skill level. Practice every day for 15 minutes minimum.

Reading 12 books this year. Read 6 books. Read one book this month, the one I've been wanting to read.

Financial Goals:

Opening up a small business. Have completed the following for small business; Business plan completed, utilize business assistance and training, choose a location for business, financing for business, determine legal structure of business, register business name, get a tax ID number, register for local and state taxes, get business licenses and any permits, and know employer responsibilities. First month take action on first 3 steps; business plan completed, utilize business assistance and training, choose a location for business.

Employing 6 people. This goal may be employing 2 people at the six month point, depending on whether or not the establishment is up and running.

Give 3% of personal earnings to my favorite non-profit organization. This can remain the same, give 3% of personal earnings to my favorite non-profit organization. This can remain the same, give 3% of personal earnings to my favorite non-profit organization.

Spiritual Goals

Volunteering at a Hospital. This can remain the same at the six month mark, can be volunteering at a hospital. Find a hospital to volunteer. Complete any requirements that may be asked.

Tithing to my church 10%. This can remain the same at 6 months. Start tithing 10%.

Writing and journaling every night for 15 minutes before going to sleep. This can remain the same at 6 months. Begin journaling this month, this week. Purchase Swimming in the Goodness Journal to write down nightly positive daily actions, positive behaviors, goals accomplished, and even write down new goals or actions required for remaining successful. Write down any new dreams, positive affirmations, or things to do. Then fall to sleep peaceful, relaxed, happy, and content.

Meditating and praying throughout the day. This can remain the same at 6 months. Each morning this month I can begin to meditate 5 minutes in the morning. Look on line for different breathing exercises, find one that I really like and that feels comfortable and then do it for 5 minutes the first several weeks. Try another breathing exercise if wanted, and then apply that breathing technique each morning for 10 minutes if possible. 5 minutes is fine until I am ready for 10 minutes. Do the same with praying. Throughout my day I can do these to stay centered and happy.

Emotional Goals

Becoming more serene, confident, and hanging around happy people. This can remain the same at 6 months. Do deep breathing exercise to increase oxygen to brain creating more calmness and confidence. Find meet-up groups or organizations that do things that I would like to do and become a part of that group. Being supported and supporting others is powerful.

Developing stronger and healthier habits. This can remain the same at 6 months. Not yelling when angry. This month be disciplined in diet and workout routine. Read an empowering book. Listen to empowering, positive, and encouraging video's on YouTube. Tell myself 10 positive things that I love about myself each day this week.

Social Goals

Getting involved and taking on a leadership role in my favorite organization. This can remain the same at 6 months. Choose an organization if not already involved in one and learn the various roles and responsibilities. Go once a week to partake in meetings or events.

Dancing with friends often. This can remain the same at 6 months. Call up friends and set up the venue to go check out this weekend. Once a month would be cool.

Volunteer for city fun run. This can remain the same at 6 months. <u>Sign up for upcoming fun run as a volunteer. Run the race too if allowed.</u>

Have a strong business network. This can remain the same at 6 months. <u>Research on the web local networking groups, make contact and attend the next upcoming meeting.</u>

Personal Goals

Take a family vacation to Colorado during the winter and ski. Have chosen the Hotel, ski resort, or cabin 2 months before Dec. 17. <u>Find a ski resort in Colorado best for family vacation. Aspen, Copper Mountain, or Crested Butte. Find out lift ticket costs and packages.</u>

Surf getaway in Costa Rica. Get the friend list request written, choose the hotel or house rental and paid for by 2 months out, know of night life hot spots, events, and other must do's.

Help mentor young adults on living abundant lives. Join an organization that helps youth in the community. <u>Book completed and published. Have feed-back from 50 people. Setting up events or seminars to promote book to help youth. Talking with business owners and bookstores to sell book in their store.</u>

Being a better parent and be more present by listening and spending quality time with children. Set aside 30 minutes a day for children to connect on a deeper level and to be more present.

Cliff jumping into the ocean. Find the cliff jumping spots in Costa Rica and any nearby beaches. Also locate any other great cliff jumping beaches and plan a small trip with family and a few friends.

To conclude the purpose of writing down our monthly goals, it is in this step that our long range goals become clear. The idea of this Golden Guide is to provide direction and more importantly create movement and action. By being directed by our long term goals, we have tangible, workable, and doable actions. We can now take these monthly goals that ensure living our dreams and ambitions. Each phase in our timeline serves a purpose. In order to swim in the goodness, we have to know that it is all around us. It is here for us to have, to experience, and to enjoy. Your action is the key to unlocking the door of your dreams.

Weekly Goals

Weekly goals is a fundamental aspect to Swimming in the Goodness! It is in our weekly activities that this dream chasing really becomes possible. Look at what you do currently on a weekly basis. Where are those actions taking you? Is it bringing you any closer to living out your dreams that lay dormant within you? It is clear at this stage to see how important it is to utilize the time in each of the 7 days of a week. What we decide to do this week will have a lasting impact on our tomorrow's.

This is an exciting phase of this Golden Guide to Swimming in the Goodness. This is where we begin to see the possibilities come to life. This is where hope becomes touchable. This is where we begin to feel and believe that this really is possible. Continuing on with our example goals for each of the seven areas of goal setting, the designated writing will be in **BOLD** to define our weekly goals.

Remember, italics is our year goal, normal font is our 6 month goal, and underlines sentences are our monthly goals.

Physical goals

Weigh 146 pounds and be healthy, lean, and fit. Weigh 159 pounds and be healthy, lean and fit at the six month point. *Workout 5 days a week.* Workout 4 days a week. <u>Weigh 170 pounds by the end of the month.</u> <u>Work out 3 days a week for this first month.</u> <u>Eat clean meals (Breakfast, lunch and dinner including all snacks) 3 days out of the week minimum.</u> **This week I will workout for 10 minutes at the gym for 3 days. Next week for four days 10 minutes. Third week 5 days 15 minutes. Fourth week 5 days 30 minutes.**

Have a massage once a month. <u>This goal stays the same.</u> **This week I will schedule an appointment for next week.**

Hike the Great Himalaya Trail, Nepal. Have the trip planned out by this point. Know who is going on the trip, the dates of the trip, costs involved, the payment due dates for flight, transportation, and stay accommodations. <u>Decide date for Nepal hiking trip. Send out invitation to friends asking them to confirm within three weeks if they are interested in going on hiking trip.</u> **This week I will send out the invitation for the Nepal Trip.**

Mental goals:

Completing this year of schooling with a minimum of a 3.7 gpa. This semester I will take 3 courses instead of 4, study more by myself and in study groups with classmates, and spend 3 hours a week getting tutored. **This week I will register at school.**

Learn Spanish. Take a Spanish course. <u>Register for upcoming Spanish course.</u> **This week I will register at school and make one of the classes a Spanish course.**

Play on piano Ludwig Van Beethoven's Fur Elise. Set aside a minimum of 20 minutes a day for playing piano. <u>Find a piano teacher and start taking piano lessons by next week to improve skill level. Practice every day for 15 minutes minimum.</u> **Begin taking lessons this week with my instructor.**

Reading 12 books this year. Read 6 books. <u>Read one book this month, the one I've been wanting to read.</u> **Go to bookstore and buy that book I've been wanting to read and I'll read 30 minutes each day. I did watch an hour and a half of television each day, only an hour a day now.**

Financial Goals:

Opening up a small business. Have completed the following for small business; Business plan completed, utilize business assistance and training, choose a location for business, financing for business, determine legal structure of business, register business name, get a tax ID number, register for local and state taxes, get business licenses and any permits, and know employer responsibilities. First month take action on first 3 steps; business plan completed, utilize business assistance and training, choose a location for business. **Start and complete business plan this week.**

Employing 6 people. This goal may be employing 2 people at the six month point, depending on whether or not the establishment is up and running.

Give 3% of personal earnings to my favorite non-profit organization. This can remain the same, give 3% of personal earnings to my favorite non-profit organization. This can remain the same, give 3% of personal earnings to my favorite non-profit organization. **Figure out the organization I would like to donate to this week.**

Spiritual Goals

Volunteering at a Hospital. This can remain the same at the six month mark, can be volunteering at a hospital. Find a hospital to volunteer. Complete any requirements that may be asked. **Go to the help desk at the local hospital and find out how to volunteer for 4 hours two weeks out of the month.**

Tithing to my church 10%. This can remain the same at 6 months. Start tithing 10%. **This week's pay day give 10% for my church online.**

Writing and journaling every night for 15 minutes before going to sleep. This can remain the same at 6 months. Begin journaling this month, this week. Purchase Swimming in the Goodness Journal to write down nightly positive daily actions, positive behaviors, goals accomplished, and even write down new goals or actions required for remaining successful. Write down any new dreams, positive affirmations, or things to do. Then fall to sleep peaceful, relaxed, happy, and content. **This week**

purchase Swimming in the Goodness Journal and start writing nightly 5 to 15 minutes about the joys and accomplishments of the day.

Meditating and praying throughout the day. This can remain the same at 6 months. Each morning this month I can begin to meditate 5 minutes in the morning. Look on line for different breathing exercises, find one that I really like and that feels comfortable and then do it for 5 minutes the first several weeks. Try another breathing exercise if wanted, and then apply that breathing technique each morning for 10 minutes if possible. 5 minutes is fine until I am ready for 10 minutes. Do the same with praying. Throughout my day I can do these to stay centered and happy. **This week I will look online for a breathing exercise to commit to and do in the morning, even midday too.**

Emotional Goals

Becoming more serene, confident, and hanging around happy people. This can remain the same at 6 months. Do deep breathing exercise to increase oxygen to brain creating more calmness and confidence. Find meet-up groups or organizations that do things that I would like to do and become a part of that group. Being supported and supporting others is powerful. **This week I will find a group of people that run so I can join them and be around like-minded people and meet new friends. I will also tell myself 10 things that I love about myself.**

Developing stronger and healthier habits. This can remain the same at 6 months. Not yelling when angry. This month be disciplined in diet and workout routine. Read an empowering book. Listen to empowering, positive, and encouraging video's on Youtube. Tell myself 10 positive things that I love about myself each day this week. **This week I will listen to a positive and encouraging YouTube video while I cook breakfast.**

Social Goals

Getting involved and taking on a leadership role in my favorite organization. This can remain the same at 6 months. Choose an organization if not already involved in one and learn the various roles and responsibilities. Go once a week to partake in meetings or events. **This week I will look into** various community organizations and find one that fits right with me. **Toastmasters International or National Speaker Association.**

Dancing with friends often. This can remain the same at 6 months. Call up friends and set up the venue to go check out this weekend. Once a month would be cool. **This week see which bands or artists that are coming into town.**

Volunteer for cities Fun Run. This can remain the same at 6 months. Sign up for upcoming fun run as a volunteer. Run the race too if allowed. **Sign up this week for next local Fun Run.**

Have a strong business network. This can remain the same at 6 months. Research on the web local networking groups, make contact and attend the next upcoming meeting. **Search this week for a business network group.**

Personal Goals

Take a family vacation to Colorado during the winter and ski. Have chosen the Hotel, ski resort, or cabin 2 months before Dec. 17. Find a ski resort in Colorado best for family vacation. Aspen, Copper Mountain, or Crested Butte. Find out lift ticket costs and packages. **This week find out costs for flight, hotels/cabins, and lift tickets. Also see any local attractions costs or concerts that may be in town.**

Surf getaway in Costa Rica. Get the friend list request written, choose the hotel or house rental and paid for by 2 months out, know of night life hot spots, events, and other must do's. **Reach out to friend's and inquire who would be interested on going to Costa Rica for a surf trip.**

Help mentor young adults on living abundant lives. Join an organization that helps youth in the community. Book completed and published. Have feed-back from 50 people. Setting up events or seminars to promote book to help youth. Talking with business owners and bookstores to sell book in their store. **This week I will have completed book. Find editor and publisher.**

Being a better parent and be more present by listening and spending quality time with children. Set aside 30 minutes a day for children to connect on a deeper level and to be more present. **This week I will ask what they would like to do for fun and do it with them, meanwhile giving my undivided attention to them.**

Cliff jumping into the ocean. Find the cliff jumping spots in Costa Rica and any nearby beaches. Also locate any other great cliff jumping beaches and plan a small trip with family and a few friends. **This task I can do 3 weeks from now (low priority).**

As you have just read, the steps break everything down to realistic actions that can be done this week. Most of these tasks will barely scratch the surface of the time within your whole day. Will it take time to pursue and attain your dreams, absolutely! We have to be willing to do the actions necessary to live our dreams. Remember that it is a blueprint, so enjoy the process of attaining your dreams. Have an exciting and joyful attitude during this phase. This practice should be fun and inspiring. If it is not, perhaps you ought to reevaluate your goals and dreams. Are they your dreams or your friends? Are you putting too much pressure on making your dreams happen so you seem overburdened?

Swimming in the Goodness Golden Guide is the blueprint that makes reaching and living our goals possible. To live an amazing and extraordinary life, it takes direction and steady manageable action. Movement is key. You have to move your ass in order to step into your dream. Your dream already exists. It is already there. You can see it and smell it, taste it, and feel it. Look at your dream as a ballroom. You can see the door. It is our job to open the door and walk in. Your dreams await your presence. Enter the door of your dream and Swim in that Goodness! Make the actions of each week practical and appropriate. It should be fun in accomplishing each of the various small steps of each dream.

Daily Goals

Daily Goals is where we make results. What we choose to do during this day, during this moment, is what will shape and create our destiny. Our tomorrows are what we have to look forward to. It is with this day at hand that we get to use consciously or unconsciously. With purpose and direction or with idleness and aimlessness. The power is within you. The power is what we are able to use, if we choose to. Swimming in the Goodness is an option in life. It is a mindset and an attitude that can be experienced by making the conscious decision to cultivate an amazing life.

Power. Allow this word to soak into your core and be really understood. Look in a hardback Webster's Dictionary and look at each of the meanings. Understand the many synonyms of the word power. You harness an unbelievable energy that is a dynamic power. This guide of Swimming in the Goodness is a method to utilize this power and create an extraordinary existence. It all starts with our daily choices. Stay diligent each day and enjoy your rewards. Be in action, stay in movement, and do the tasks of the day. Do not overburden your 24 hours. Allow yourself time to breathe and enjoy life meanwhile staying true to your dreams and ambitions!

Our actions on our daily to-do list have been derived from a long term range, from a goal, a dream, and an ambition that resides within us. Each dream in each area of your life has been written down. It is here where you take the action to see them come into being. Manifesting your dreams is not as difficult as you once may have believed. So below are examples of our long range goals reduced from 10 years out, to five years, to one year, six months, monthly, weekly, and to this day. Below the daily goals are written in bold, italics, and underline called "Today's Actions." Remember, this is just a glimpse of today. There are six other days that will fill in action steps to complete this week's goals.

Physical goals:

Weigh 146 pounds and be healthy, lean, and fit. Weigh 159 pounds and be healthy, lean and fit at the six month point. *Workout 5 days a week.* Workout 4 days a week. <u>Weigh 170 pounds by the end of the month. Work out 3 days a week for this first month. Eat clean meals (Breakfast, lunch and dinner including all snacks) 3 days out of the week minimum.</u> **This week I will workout** for 10 minutes at the gym for 3 days. Next week for four days 10 minutes. Third week 5 days 15 minutes. Fourth week 5 days 30 minutes.

Today's Action: Go to gym after work for a ten minute cardio workout and then stretch afterwards.

Have a massage once a month. This goal stays the same. **This week I will schedule an appointment for next week.**

Hike the Great Himalaya Trail, Nepal. Have the trip planned out by this point. Know who is going on the trip, the dates of the trip, costs involved, the payment due dates for flight, transportation, and stay accommodations. Decide date for Nepal hiking trip. Send out invitation to friends asking them to confirm within three weeks if they are interested in going on hiking trip. **This week I will send out the invitation for the Nepal Trip.**

Mental goals:

Completing this year of schooling with a minimum of a 3.7 gpa. This semester I will take 3 courses instead of 4, study more by myself and in study groups with classmates, and spend 3 hours a week getting tutored. **This week I will register at school.**

Today's Action: Register for school.

Learn Spanish. Take a Spanish course. Register for upcoming Spanish course. **This week I will register at school and make one of the classes a Spanish course.**

Play on piano Ludwig Van Beethoven's Fur Elise. Set aside a minimum of 20 minutes a day for playing piano. Find a piano teacher and start taking piano lessons by next week to improve skill level. Practice every day for 15 minutes minimum. **Begin taking lessons this week with my instructor.**

Reading 12 books this year. Read 6 books. <u>Read one book this month, the one I've been wanting to read.</u> **Go to bookstore and buy that book I've been wanting to read and I'll read 30 minutes each day. I watch an hour and a half of television each day, only an hour now.**

Today's Action: Stop by bookstore and pick up book.

Financial Goals:

Opening up a small business. Have completed the following for small business; Business plan completed, utilize business assistance and training, choose a location for business, financing for business, determine legal structure of business, register business name, get a tax ID number, register for local and state taxes, get business licenses and any permits, and know employer responsibilities. <u>First month take action on first 3 steps; business plan completed, utilize business assistance and training, choose a location for business.</u> **Start and complete business plan this week.**

Employing 6 people. This goal may be employing 2 people at the six month point, depending on whether or not the establishment is up and running.

Give 3% of personal earnings to my favorite non-profit organization. This can remain the same, give 3% of personal earnings to my favorite non-profit organization. <u>This can remain the same, give 3% of personal earnings to my favorite non-profit organization.</u> **Figure out the organization I would like to donate to this week.**

Spiritual Goals

Volunteering at a Hospital. This can remain the same at the six month mark, can be volunteering at a hospital. <u>Find a hospital to volunteer. Complete any requirements that may be asked.</u> **Go to the help desk at the local hospital and find out how to volunteer for 4 hours two weeks out of the month.**

Tithing to my church 10%. This can remain the same at 6 months. <u>Start tithing 10%.</u> **This week's pay day give 10% for my church online.**

Writing and journaling every night for 15 minutes before going to sleep. This can remain the same at 6 months. <u>Begin journaling this month, this week. Purchase Swimming in the Goodness Journal to write down nightly positive daily actions, positive behaviors, goals accomplished, and even write down new goals or actions required for remaining successful. Write down any new dreams, positive affirmations, or things to do. Then fall to sleep peaceful, relaxed, happy, and content.</u> **This week purchase Swimming in the Goodness Journal and start writing nightly 5 to 15 minutes about the joys and accomplishments of the day.**

<u>Daily Action: Before retiring for the night, journal of today's successes and things that I am grateful for.</u>

Meditating and praying throughout the day. This can remain the same at 6 months. <u>Each morning this month I can begin to meditate 5 minutes in the morning. Look on line for different breathing exercises, find one that I really like and that feels comfortable and then do it for 5 minutes the first several weeks. Try another breathing exercise if wanted, and then apply that breathing technique each morning for 10 minutes if possible. 5 minutes is fine until I am ready for 10 minutes. Do the same with praying. Throughout my day I can do these to stay centered and happy.</u> **This week I will look online for a breathing exercise to commit to and do in the morning, even mid-day too.**

<u>Daily Action: Find a breathing exercise for tomorrow morning.</u>

Emotional Goals

Becoming more serene, confident, and hanging around happy people. This can remain the same at 6 months. <u>Do the deep breathing exercise to increase oxygen to brain creating more calmness and confidence. Find meet-up groups or organizations that do things that I would like to do and become a part of that group. Being supported and supporting others is powerful.</u> **This week I will** find a group of people that run so I can join them and be around like minded people and meet new friends. I will also tell myself 10 things that I love about myself.

Daily Action: Say aloud ten things that I love about myself.

Developing stronger and healthier habits. This can remain the same at 6 months. Not yelling when angry. This month be disciplined in diet and workout routine. Read an empowering book. Listen to empowering, positive, and encouraging video's on YouTube. Tell myself 10 positive things that I love about myself each day this week. **This week I will listen to a positive and encouraging YouTube video while I cook breakfast.**

Social Goals

Getting involved and taking on a leadership role in my favorite organization. This can remain the same at 6 months. Choose an organization if not already involved in one and learn the various roles and responsibilities. Go once a week to partake in meetings or events. **This week I will look into various community organizations and find one that fits right with me.**

Dancing with friends often. This can remain the same at 6 months. Call up friends and set up the venue to go check out this weekend. Once a month would be cool. **This week see which bands or artists that are coming into town.**

Volunteer for cities Fun Run. This can remain the same at 6 months. Sign up for upcoming fun run as a volunteer. Run the race too if allowed. **Sign up this week for next local Fun-Run.**

Daily Action: Look up next upcoming local fun run and sign up the family.

Have a strong business network. This can remain the same at 6 months. Research on the web local networking groups, make contact and attend the next upcoming meeting. **Search this week for a business network group.**

Personal Goals

Take a family vacation to Colorado during the winter and ski. *Have chosen the* Hotel, ski resort, or cabin 2 months before Dec. 17. <u>Find a ski resort in Colorado best for family vacation.</u> <u>Aspen, Copper Mountain, or Crested Butte. Find out lift ticket costs and packages.</u> **This week find out costs for flight, hotels/cabins, and lift tickets. Also see any local attractions costs or concerts that may be in town.**

Surf getaway in Costa Rica. Get the friend list request written, choose the hotel or house rental and paid for by 2 months out, know of night life hot spots, events, and other must do's. **Reach out to friend's and inquire who would be interested on going to Costa Rica for a surf trip.**

Daily Actions: Send out email to the tribe for the Costa trip.

Help mentor young adults on living abundant lives. Book completed and published. Have feedback from 50 people. Setting up events or seminars to promote book. Have done 100 events promoting book to help people live abundant lives. Talking with business owners and bookstores to sell book in their store. **This week I will have completed book. Find editor and publisher.**

Daily Actions: Write a minimum of an hour today.

Being a better parent and be more present by listening and spending quality time with children. Set aside 30 minutes a day for children to connect on a deeper level and to be more present. **This week I will ask what they would like to do for fun and do it with them, meanwhile giving my undivided attention to them.**

Daily Actions: Spend time after dinner with kids and ask them about their day, how they are feeling and what new things happened today.

Cliff jumping into the ocean. Find the cliff jumping spots in Costa Rica and any nearby beaches. Also locate any other great cliff jumping beaches and plan a small trip with family and a few friends. **This task I can do 3 weeks from now (low priority).**

To conclude our Daily Goals category, we can see how in the illustrated 24 hour day period, there are only ten ***Today's Actions*** that were written down. This is a very manageable daily to-do list. This very simple to-do list is the platform, the foundation for you to create the experience of your dreams. For an experience that genuinely is amazing and extraordinary. Can you do ten tasks today that will help you Swim in the Goodness? Absolutely you can!

Movement, action, consistency, and purpose are all fundamental ingredients to living our dreams. Joy, passion, positive attitudes, and positive thinking are keys when embarking on creating our lives. Your destiny and your dreams are yours. Enjoy them and embrace your power of shaping an amazing and extraordinary experience. Do today only the things that need to be done. If you have more time available and are able to take on a few more tasks that will contribute to your accomplishing your goals, then do them. So long as it is not distressing and creating misery.

Lastly, love your life, love your experience, right here right now. No matter your circumstance or current environment, you are the master of your destiny. Own yourself and take action and responsibility. By doing this we can help others. By taking ownership of ourselves, we become magnetic and attractive to others. Be that light that shines brightly and boldly. Be the person that gives hope to others that a great life is possible. Be that for yourself first. Swimming in the Goodness is exactly as the title states. This book is a guide to living an amazing and extraordinary life where your dreams and inner gold become your reality.

The Essence of Time

The essence of time is invaluable. Time is the rarest gift that we have. Time is often misunderstood. Swimming in the Goodness, the Golden Guide provides a system that we can apply to heighten our opportunity to swim in the goodness. This book will stimulate the desire to be more efficient with our time and our energy in all aspects of our lives. You will become accomplished and satisfied. It's a continuous process of growing and expanding. Creating experiences that are pleasurable, joyful, and beautiful is the point of life. So the next time a friend, acquaintance, or stranger asks you, "How have you been?" You may respond with a smile, "Swimming in the Goodness!"

Swimming in the Goodness

How often do we hear an older person say that if they had the opportunity to do things differently that they would? Perhaps even you yourself have said those words and wished you would have done things differently. Regardless of your age, Swimming in the Goodness is the catalyst for any person young or old, to take charge of their own life. This book is not about comparing ourselves to others, putting others on a pedestal, or looking outside of ourselves for satisfaction. The next several chapters is for you to sit quietly, dream, and put down on paper the experiences that you wish to live. You can also do this as a family or in a group. Having like-minded people support you as you support their dreams and aspirations is uplifting. The point is to get in touch with our own individual dreams.

Who are we lying to if we choose to not live out our dreams and desires? Who are we hurting by not allowing our truth to shine? Ourselves. This Golden Guide to Swimming in the Goodness allows us to shine, to be free and fulfilled, and imbued with a glow of passion and purpose. Passion and purpose that we find within our own hearts and minds. Now, we may see others having an experience that we ourselves would like to experience. This is perfectly fine and normal. Write down that desire or aspiration as a goal of yours. Be realistic on the time frame.

For example, you see a person being helicoptered into an Alaskan mountain peak. They commence to ski down the face of a mountain fresh with powdered snow. If you never have skied before, put as an immediate goal, learning how to ski by taking lessons prior to standing on top of an Alaskan Mountain Peak. Funny I know. Then set goals of graduating to higher levels of skills. Doing something outside of our level of understanding can be detrimental.

Another example may be seeing a person make a meal that looks pretty tasty. If the meal is in alignment with our overall Physical Goals, then make that meal the same night. We can do things in their own time as we are ready to experience them. What is important to know at this time is that we create our lives. We decide what we are willing to do and not do. We choose if we are going to allow an experience to happen. This is all in regards to writing down our dreams and aspirations now. Life does happen and we all have to make adjustments along the way. Just make the necessary adjustments along the way.

Swimming in the Goodness

As this portion of the book comes to it conclusion, we are better equipped with understanding the Swimming in the Goodness principles provided by this Golden Guide. What follows this portion of the book is the application section of the book. What ensues will be seven chapters that cover all areas of goal setting in all time milestones. This by no means has to be completed in one sitting. This can take several days or even weeks for some of you to completely fill out the written section of this book. Some people may have many goals in every area. While other people may have stronger dreams in fewer areas. Whatever your inner treasures may be, have fun and smile, be alive! Write them down and know there is purpose, hope, and love all around you. Those treasures await you as much as you await them!

CHAPTER 3

10 YEAR GOALS

This is the section of the book where you put a pen in hand and write down your dreams, ambitions, goals, and desires. It is strongly recommended that you allow yourself to dream boldly. Think of all the things that you would like to see yourself doing in ten years from now. Nothing holds us back except ourselves. So at this time, you are removed from any blockages and obstacles, and are able to see and feel joy. Money is not an obstacle either when writing down your dreams.

See and feel the joy that you would be feeling while living that dream. Where you would like to be living, doing what you would like to be doing, and what you would like to be earning. You are the writer of your life! Swim in the Goodness!

10 Year Physical Goals

_____

_____

_____

_____

_____

_____

_____

_____

_____

_____

_____

_____

_____

_____

_____

_____

_____

_____

_____

_____

_____

_____

_____

_____

_____

_____

10 Year Mental Goals

_____

_____

_____

_____

_____

_____

_____

_____

_____

_____

_____

_____

_____

_____

_____

_____

_____

_____

_____

_____

_____

_____

_____

_____

_____

_____

_____

_____

_____

10 Year Financial Goals

_____

_____

_____

_____

_____

_____

_____

_____

_____

_____

_____

_____

_____

_____

_____

_____

_____

_____

_____

_____

_____

_____

_____

_____

_____

_____

_____

_____

10 Year Spiritual Goals

_____

_____

_____

_____

_____

_____

_____

_____

_____

_____

_____

_____

_____

_____

_____

_____

_____

_____

_____

_____

_____

_____

_____

_____

_____

_____

_____

_____

10 Year Emotional Goals

_____
_____
_____
_____
_____
_____
_____
_____
_____
_____
_____
_____
_____
_____
_____
_____
_____
_____
_____
_____
_____
_____
_____
_____
_____
_____
_____
_____
_____

10 Year Social Goals

_____

_____

_____

_____

_____

_____

_____

_____

_____

_____

_____

_____

_____

_____

_____

_____

_____

_____

_____

_____

_____

_____

_____

_____

_____

_____

_____

_____

10 Year Personal Goals

_____

_____

_____

_____

_____

_____

_____

_____

_____

_____

_____

_____

_____

_____

_____

_____

_____

_____

_____

_____

_____

_____

_____

_____

_____

CHAPTER 4

5 YEAR GOALS

In this chapter, write down your five year goals. There are many dreams, ambitions, and goals that are in the five year range. Some of these goals stand alone, independent of your ten year goals. In each of the seven areas provided, write down each goal and dream regardless of how small or grand it may be.

Now look at the dreams written in the Ten Year Chapter that proceeded this chapter. What is the halfway point of each goal that you could have done by the fifth year? Figure that you have to be willing to have completed half of this work by this point of time. You will have to rewrite the next five years in five years from now to stay on course in achieving each Ten Year Goal.

Dream boldly and think of all the things that you would like to see yourself doing in five years from today. You are completely free to dream of anything and are able to write each of these thoughts down. Money is not an issue, while dreaming we have everything at our hands, and it's all ready to be utilized. It's limitless! You are the writer of your life! Swim in the Goodness!

5 Year Physical Goals

_____
_____
_____
_____
_____
_____
_____
_____
_____
_____
_____
_____
_____
_____
_____
_____
_____
_____
_____
_____
_____
_____
_____
_____
_____
_____
_____
_____
_____

5 Year Mental Goals

_____

_____

_____

_____

_____

_____

_____

_____

_____

_____

_____

_____

_____

_____

_____

_____

_____

_____

_____

_____

_____

_____

_____

_____

_____

_____

_____

_____

5 Year Financial Goals

_____

_____

_____

_____

_____

_____

_____

_____

_____

_____

_____

_____

_____

_____

_____

_____

_____

_____

_____

_____

_____

_____

_____

_____

_____

Swimming in the Goodness

5 Year Spiritual Goals

5 Year Emotional Goals

_____

_____

_____

_____

_____

_____

_____

_____

_____

_____

_____

_____

_____

_____

_____

_____

_____

_____

_____

_____

_____

_____

_____

_____

_____

5 Year Social Goals

_____

_____

_____

_____

_____

_____

_____

_____

_____

_____

_____

_____

_____

_____

_____

_____

_____

_____

_____

_____

_____

_____

_____

_____

_____

_____

5 Year Personal Goals

CHAPTER 5

1 YEAR GOALS

In this chapter review the five year goals. We have five individual years to direct our actions. By dividing each five year goal into five yearly goals, we can manage the achievement of each dream much easier. It is important that you break down each goal into 5 simple steps. Assign the first year the first step. Do this same technique for every goal and dream that you written in the previous chapter. We focus our energy on the first year only for the purpose of Swimming in the Goodness. There is a workbook that is refined for One Year Goals to daily goals. It will be important to have a copy when entering the final quarter of this first year of goal setting. This will give you ample time to review each five year goal. Then you can check your progress. Make any necessary adjustments. Finally, write down the second year goals and actions in your new workbook.

1 Year Physical Goals

_____

_____

_____

_____

_____

_____

_____

_____

_____

_____

_____

_____

_____

_____

_____

_____

_____

_____

_____

_____

_____

_____

_____

_____

_____

_____

_____

1 Year Mental Goals

_____

_____

_____

_____

_____

_____

_____

_____

_____

_____

_____

_____

_____

_____

_____

_____

_____

_____

_____

_____

_____

_____

_____

_____

_____

_____

_____

_____

1 Year Financial Goals

_____

_____

_____

_____

_____

_____

_____

_____

_____

_____

_____

_____

_____

_____

_____

_____

_____

_____

_____

_____

_____

_____

_____

_____

_____

_____

1 Year Spiritual Goals

1 Year Emotional Goals

_____
_____
_____
_____
_____
_____
_____
_____
_____
_____
_____
_____
_____
_____
_____
_____
_____
_____
_____
_____
_____
_____
_____
_____
_____
_____
_____

Swimming in the Goodness

1 Year Social Goals

_____

_____

_____

_____

_____

_____

_____

_____

_____

_____

_____

_____

_____

_____

_____

_____

_____

_____

_____

_____

_____

_____

_____

_____

_____

_____

1 Year Personal Goals

_____

_____

_____

_____

_____

_____

_____

_____

_____

_____

_____

_____

_____

_____

_____

_____

_____

_____

_____

_____

_____

_____

_____

_____

6 MONTH GOALS

Review the yearly goals and in this chapter, divide each yearly goal in half. Write down half of the steps that would be required in order to be at the midpoint in six months from now.

6 Month Physical Goals

_____

_____

_____

_____

_____

_____

_____

_____

_____

_____

_____

_____

_____

_____

_____

_____

_____

_____

_____

_____

_____

_____

_____

_____

_____

6 Month Mental Goals

_____
_____
_____
_____
_____
_____
_____
_____
_____
_____
_____
_____
_____
_____
_____
_____
_____
_____
_____
_____
_____
_____
_____
_____
_____
_____
_____

6 Month Financial Goals

_____

_____

_____

_____

_____

_____

_____

_____

_____

_____

_____

_____

_____

_____

_____

_____

_____

_____

_____

_____

_____

_____

_____

_____

_____

_____

_____

_____

_____

_____

_____

_____

6 Month Spiritual Goals

6 Month Emotional Goals

_____
_____
_____
_____
_____
_____
_____
_____
_____
_____
_____
_____
_____
_____
_____
_____
_____
_____
_____
_____
_____
_____
_____
_____
_____

6 Month Social Goals

_____
_____
_____
_____
_____
_____
_____
_____
_____
_____
_____
_____
_____
_____
_____
_____
_____
_____
_____
_____
_____
_____
_____
_____

6 Month Personal Goals

CHAPTER 7

MONTHLY GOALS

Review each six month goal and break down each goal into six manageable steps. For the Purpose of this book, write down the first month goals in the next section provided.

This Month's Physical Goals

_____

_____

_____

_____

_____

_____

_____

_____

_____

_____

_____

_____

_____

_____

_____

_____

_____

_____

_____

_____

_____

_____

_____

_____

This Month's Mental Goals

_____

_____

_____

_____

_____

_____

_____

_____

_____

_____

_____

_____

_____

_____

_____

_____

_____

_____

_____

_____

_____

_____

_____

_____

_____

_____

This Month's Financial Goals

_____

_____

_____

_____

_____

_____

_____

_____

_____

_____

_____

_____

_____

_____

_____

_____

_____

_____

_____

_____

_____

_____

_____

_____

Swimming in the Goodness

This Month's Spiritual Goals

_____

_____

_____

_____

_____

_____

_____

_____

_____

_____

_____

_____

_____

_____

_____

_____

_____

_____

_____

_____

_____

_____

_____

Swimming in the Goodness

This Month's Emotional Goals

This Month's Social Goals

_____
_____
_____
_____
_____
_____
_____
_____
_____
_____
_____
_____
_____
_____
_____
_____
_____
_____
_____
_____
_____
_____
_____
_____
_____

This Month's Personal Goals

_____

_____

_____

_____

_____

_____

_____

_____

_____

_____

_____

_____

_____

_____

_____

_____

_____

_____

_____

_____

_____

_____

_____

_____

_____

_____

_____

_____

CHAPTER 8

WEEKLY GOALS

With every monthly goal, divide each monthly goal into 4 steps. Designate the first step for week one, the second step for week two, and so on. In any month that has a fifth week, take advantage of that extra week and keep your progress moving forward.

This Week's Physical Goals

_____

_____

_____

_____

_____

_____

_____

_____

_____

_____

_____

_____

_____

_____

_____

_____

_____

_____

_____

_____

_____

_____

_____

_____

_____

This Week's Mental Goals

_____

_____

_____

_____

_____

_____

_____

_____

_____

_____

_____

_____

_____

_____

_____

_____

_____

_____

_____

_____

_____

_____

_____

_____

_____

This Week's Financial Goals

_____

_____

_____

_____

_____

_____

_____

_____

_____

_____

_____

_____

_____

_____

_____

_____

_____

_____

_____

_____

_____

_____

_____

_____

This Week's Spiritual Goals

This Week's Emotional Goals

_____

_____

_____

_____

_____

_____

_____

_____

_____

_____

_____

_____

_____

_____

_____

_____

_____

_____

_____

_____

_____

_____

_____

_____

This Week's Social Goals

_____

_____

_____

_____

_____

_____

_____

_____

_____

_____

_____

_____

_____

_____

_____

_____

_____

_____

_____

_____

_____

_____

_____

_____

This Week's Personal Goals

_____

_____

_____

_____

_____

_____

_____

_____

_____

_____

_____

_____

_____

_____

_____

_____

_____

_____

_____

_____

_____

_____

_____

_____

_____

CHAPTER 9

DAILY GOALS

In this chapter, we review the first week's goals. Structure the next seven days so that this week is effective, rewarding, and enjoyable.

Today's Physical Goals

_____

_____

_____

_____

_____

_____

_____

_____

_____

_____

_____

_____

_____

_____

_____

_____

_____

_____

_____

_____

_____

_____

_____

_____

_____

_____

_____

Today's Mental Goals

_____

_____

_____

_____

_____

_____

_____

_____

_____

_____

_____

_____

_____

_____

_____

_____

_____

_____

_____

_____

_____

_____

_____

_____

_____

_____

_____

Today's Financial Goals

_____

_____

_____

_____

_____

_____

_____

_____

_____

_____

_____

_____

_____

_____

_____

_____

_____

_____

_____

_____

_____

_____

_____

_____

_____

_____

Today's Spiritual Goals

_____

_____

_____

_____

_____

_____

_____

_____

_____

_____

_____

_____

_____

_____

_____

_____

_____

_____

_____

_____

_____

_____

_____

_____

Today's Emotional Goals

Today's Social Goals

Today's Personal Goals

CHAPTER 10

ADDITIONAL CRITERIA

The following pages will help refine your dreams, passions, and ambitions. After writing out this section, return to the Goal Section of this book and add any information that you may have forgotten. For now, write down anything that comes to mind. Write them down openly, as if money were not a concern. What would you want to experience and do by yourself, with your family, with your friends? How would you look? How would you feel? How would you get there?

It is important to see it and feel it! You are already Swimming in the Goodness. All we are doing is changing our environment or rather, changing the Goodness that we are Swimming in. So be true and honest with yourself here. Remember, these are your dreams and beautiful thoughts that are yours!

Places I'd like to Go

Dream Home

_____

_____

_____

_____

_____

_____

_____

_____

_____

_____

_____

_____

_____

_____

_____

_____

_____

_____

_____

_____

_____

_____

_____

_____

Dream Car(s)

_____

_____

_____

_____

_____

_____

_____

_____

_____

_____

_____

_____

_____

_____

_____

_____

_____

_____

_____

_____

_____

_____

_____

_____

_____

_____

Organizations to Volunteer

_____

_____

_____

_____

_____

_____

_____

_____

_____

_____

_____

_____

_____

_____

_____

_____

_____

_____

_____

_____

_____

_____

_____

_____

Things I would like to have (Toys)

My Strengths

_____

_____

_____

_____

_____

_____

_____

_____

_____

_____

_____

_____

_____

_____

_____

_____

_____

_____

_____

_____

_____

_____

_____

_____

My Weaknesses

_____

_____

_____

_____

_____

_____

_____

_____

_____

_____

_____

_____

_____

_____

_____

_____

_____

_____

_____

_____

_____

_____

_____

_____

_____

Quotes that move me

_____

_____

_____

_____

_____

_____

_____

_____

_____

_____

_____

_____

_____

_____

_____

_____

_____

_____

_____

_____

_____

_____

_____

_____

_____

_____

Spouse/partner strengths or type of person I'd like to be with

People who inspire me and their strengths

Diet Interests

_____

_____

_____

_____

_____

_____

_____

_____

_____

_____

_____

_____

_____

_____

_____

_____

_____

_____

_____

_____

_____

_____

_____

Exercise Interests

_____

_____

_____

_____

_____

_____

_____

_____

_____

_____

_____

_____

_____

_____

_____

_____

_____

_____

_____

_____

_____

_____

_____

_____

_____

Not To-Do list (Things I should change)

List of Good books

_____

_____

_____

_____

_____

_____

_____

_____

_____

_____

_____

_____

_____

_____

_____

_____

_____

_____

_____

_____

_____

_____

_____

_____

_____

_____

Personal Passions

CHAPTER 11

DOCUMENTING RESULTS

As time progresses and the days turn into weeks and months, you will see many accomplishments. Each task completed gets you closer to your goal. As you hit certain milestones, write down the tasks attained. Write down every ambition, dream, or goal achieved or experienced. By writing the acquired dream or goal that has been experienced, you get to see the ground that you covered and be happy. Enjoy the progress that you have made and stay diligent in your forward movement.

Movement is essential! Take action! As we write our accomplishments, we list them and continue moving forward. In the previous sections, highlight the dreams and goals accomplished. If you prefer, place a checkmark in front of the goal attained. It's best to highlight each dream attained or experienced and then write it down in thus section of the book.

People who you may admire, most likely have a vision board. They have their goals written in some form or another. Swimming in the Goodness is the book that is here for you to reach your own heights. Swimming in the Goodness Golden Guide is a practice that directly places you ahead in life. Imagine yourself seven years from now after having lived so many dreams. Feel the joy and success in that. That my friend is attractive and powerful. That is some serious Swimming in the Goodness!

Swimming in the Goodness

In this chapter, write down all dreams that come into fruition. Periodically return to this section of the Golden Guide to get uplifted as you continue moving forward. Documenting the goals attained builds faith in this practice. It's a science that is based on cause and effect. Swimming in the Goodness the Golden Guide works. Stay disciplined on the course you have paved. Smile often, feel joy often, and share your progress with others. This will inspire others. What would really help you cover some ground would be to tell others about Swimming in the Goodness.

Tell your loved ones, friends, and even strangers about Swimming in the Goodness. This will build momentum and an energy that is irresistible and powerful. Build a group of people that you can support and that can support you.

Dreams Accomplished or Experienced

Dreams Accomplished or Experienced

_____
_____
_____
_____
_____
_____
_____
_____
_____
_____
_____
_____
_____
_____
_____
_____
_____
_____
_____
_____
_____
_____
_____
_____
_____
_____
_____
_____

Dreams Accomplished or Experienced

_____
_____
_____
_____
_____
_____
_____
_____
_____
_____
_____
_____
_____
_____
_____
_____
_____
_____
_____
_____
_____
_____
_____
_____
_____
_____

Dreams Accomplished or Experienced

_____
_____
_____
_____
_____
_____
_____
_____
_____
_____
_____
_____
_____
_____
_____
_____
_____
_____
_____
_____
_____
_____
_____
_____
_____
_____
_____
_____

Dreams Accomplished or Experienced

_____

_____

_____

_____

_____

_____

_____

_____

_____

_____

_____

_____

_____

_____

_____

_____

_____

_____

_____

_____

_____

_____

_____

_____

_____

Dreams Accomplished or Experienced

_____
_____
_____
_____
_____
_____
_____
_____
_____
_____
_____
_____
_____
_____
_____
_____
_____
_____
_____
_____
_____
_____
_____
_____
_____

Dreams Accomplished or Experienced

_____
_____
_____
_____
_____
_____
_____
_____
_____
_____
_____
_____
_____
_____
_____
_____
_____
_____
_____
_____
_____
_____
_____
_____
_____

CHAPTER 12

BEGINNING NEW GOALS

As our dream experiences accumulate, it is important that we create a new vision. At various periods of growth during this process, we may become aware of new dreams or ambitions. Write these new ideas or thoughts down. Fit them appropriately into the process that this Golden Guide offers. Begin a new quest for the next ten years out by utilizing a new book.

What happens as we live out our dreams? After time passes, particular goals may begin to lose their influence as they become regularly experienced. For instance, you purchase your "Dream Car" in four years, one year ahead of schedule. When year eight comes to pass you may have seen new vehicles that fit your idea of a Dream Car. In such a scenario, it is healthy to continue forward, dreaming, and living an amazing and extraordinary life.

There are dreams and experiences that may be quickly lived in their experience. For instance, Skydiving. Once you jump out of the airplane, it's on. You land safely and continue on with your day. Highlight that dream off of the list. Then write it down in the previous chapter of this book called Dreams Accomplished or Experienced. Then look at another ambition and do it. Let's say the next dream is to see the Northern Lights. The time arrives, you arranged your travel accommodations and see the majestic aura of the Northern Lights. Now highlight that dream off in the section where you placed it in this book. Then write it down in the Dreams Accomplished or Experienced section of the eleventh chapter. On to the next dream, it is that simple.

Perhaps you met someone in the city of your dreams who makes a suggestion for you to travel to Norway on your next vacation. Just like that, you well may have a new destination to write down. Whether it is six months out, 2 years out, or five years, the point is that you now have a new goal to experience.

Some dreams are superficial while other dreams reside in the depths of your heart. Perhaps you have dreams of helping people with medical issues such as cancer. This is a passion that can experienced for the course of your life time. Fulfill such dreams that reside in the core of your being. That is some rare Swimming in the Goodness right there! Swimming in the Goodness the Golden Guide is a design that will enable you to live out your purpose. This book is the path that will allow you to live out those dreams and ambitions that serve your higher good.

Living out such dreams and passions are rare. The reason why they are rare is because so many people find their divine desires but may not see the bridge to get there. This Golden Guide is the bridge for us to Swim in the Goodness. It is here for you to build an extraordinary experience. Our thoughts are powerful. Our thoughts that come from our hearts desires are special. That is what makes you unique. Our dreams written down become visible setting the stage to where a dynamic force is found. Movement is the catalyst for extraordinary. Action is the catalyst for amazing. As momentum increases and this force directs your path, you will see changes that will impact your life forever.

Understand the following process. Thoughts, dreams, putting those dreams on paper, taking action, inevitably creates results. Results that have led to accomplishment, cultivate a rich life full of satisfaction. Generate and regenerate dreams. Dream, experience each dream, and dream again. Everything, and I mean everything that is here is temporary. Someone comes into your life and you get to enjoy an experience with them for a day. Perhaps several years before circumstances remove them from your life. Perhaps they remain in your life for a lifetime. This is crucial to understand. The younger you are when you realize this, the better off you will be. You will cherish people and experiences more. You will have more passion and vigor for life. Putting yourself out there 100% without holding back. We only have one life to live. One life to thrive in. One life to put into everything that resides in us and leave for the rest of the world to enjoy and grow from. That is truly powerful.

Knowing that our time is precious and limited empowers and strengthens us. This understanding will encourage and inspire us. We'll reach for new heights and search into deeper areas within ourselves. Do you see? If you choose to not say to the person behind you, "Hi, how is your day?" You may never find out that his day was wonderful, that he just got a new job that he applied for. You two talk and find out that he can help out a friend of yours who was looking for a job. Something had told to say hello and you did! Six months later, you all are having a barbeque with a bunch of new friends. You all are planning to go on a trip to Costa Rica. What? Oh yes, it happens like that! Live my friend, live and do not hold anything back.

There are too many people who can benefit from what you have to offer. Simply because, you have an incredible worth! You have gifts within you that are remarkable and you can feel them inside of you. Look at them, face them, and do all those dreams and gifts. We are here to be bold, humble, confident, enduring, nurturing, and engrossed in a joy for life. As new dreams and goals come to us, we write them down. We keep moving forward and we get to experience them. It is that easy.

Be a person that takes responsibility for their life regardless of what happened in your past. Some people have childhood tragedies that can deter their course from living their dreams. Some people had addictions, had loved ones die, and have perhaps hurt others. No longer do such things have to govern your life! There are people who had childhood tragedies that still create wonderful lives for themselves. You are one of them! People do overcome addictions and create magnificent lives. If you can relate, then you are one of the success stories! There are people who had loved ones die who still create delightful lives and you are one of them. There are people who have hurt other people who made the right adjustments and changed. Still creating appealing lives and you are one of them.

What we choose to do creates our lives. In this moment we find the power for movement and action. Forgiving our past, tapping into an inner resource that is loving and good, we take action to create beautiful experiences. Now having direction and purpose that is genuine and true, we move diligently on course. The course that you have written down in Swimming in the Goodness Golden Guide!

Completion is powerful. Events coming full circle is empowering. The journey is ours to enjoy. Be open to your true passions. Enjoy freedom in its intended purpose. You are the master of your fate. Help others and come to know reward. All these things are imperative to remember. There is just something rewarding about crossing the finish line. Seeing another person we helped complete their first year of college is inspiring. Turning off the lights after a hard day's work of serving people in the restaurant that you built from the ground up is gratifying. Seeing the sparkle in your children's eyes after months of supporting them through their scholastics and athletic events is fulfilling. Having connected with them and given quality time has built children who have self-worth, self-confidence, and self-love. More importantly they know they are important. Reaching our goals is where we get to see and feel our inner smile, our joy!

Writing your dreams in this guide does take time, energy, and effort. Establishing and sustaining this habit will help you stay close to your joy. By no means does it mean that writing down everything has to happen in one sitting. This is a lifelong guide, a blueprint to your dreams. This Golden Guide is a resource that we continue to interact with once a week to keep track of our progress and to rewrite our next week's Daily Actions.

As your week comes to an end, go over the tasks completed during the week and check the completed ones off of the list. For the uncompleted tasks, rewrite each task down for the upcoming week. Sunday evenings are a great time to set aside twenty minutes and go over last week's Daily Actions. Write the new upcoming weeks Daily Actions. Once a month review some of your one year, five year, and even ten year goals. Also, document your results in the Dreams Accomplished or Experienced section of Swimming in the Goodness. This is how we stay on course, inspire ourselves, and to get renewed. We stay in the moment, focused, alert, and present. Give this time of the week to look back on your progress and then forward on your dreams and goals.

On Sunday you may also include fifteen minutes to sit on a comfortable chair, close your eyes, and do some deep breathing. Relax and visualize yourself experiencing many of your goals. The clearer you can see and feel the dream happening, the more likely that dream will come to be. When sitting and visualizing, imagine that you are actually doing and living each dream. Some dreams and goals will come easily while others may take more time. Some may be experienced quickly while others are ongoing during your lifetime.

Whatever the dream may be, visualize yourself doing the upcoming weeks tasks. See yourself talking to the people that you have to talk with. See their pleasantries, the environment that you will be in, the smells, and the success of that person saying yes to you. See that part of the puzzle to your dreams being given. See as much detail as you can as clearly as possible. Let's say that the appointment's scheduled for Wednesday at 11:00 a.m. As you walk into the building, the environment may be completely different than what you imagined in your visualization. What you are bringing though is the confidence of a favorable outcome. The result is paramount, you accomplish another task from the Daily Action for that particular week.

By spending time once a week to regroup, to get clear, and to visualize, we stay disciplined and directed. This is what it looks like for us to commit to ourselves and our dreams. This is how legacies are created. Diligent effort and continuous movement. Doing, regrouping, fine tuning, and repeat. Once a week.

Swimming in the Goodness

Not only will our energies be more efficient this way, we will find that much can be done in a twenty four hour period. Another thing that you will discover is that you will have more available time by applying yourself to this practice. Just do not over-consume yourself with too many daily tasks. Be practical and reasonable. Allow yourself to have freedom and time to have fun. Enjoyment in life outside of being focused and directed is still important. At the end of the day when you lay your head on your pillow ask yourself, did I put a genuine effort in contributing to my dreams? Meanwhile still dealing with daily life and life's on goings, were you able to be happy?

If we ask ourselves this question at night and we have an inner smile radiating, then consider that day a success. If we have an unsettling feeling, be gentle with yourself, love yourself, and make the necessary adjustments the next day. Swimming in the Goodness is a great feeling! So swim in it.

With completion comes new beginnings. Do not take yourself so seriously that you are not happy. Do not take yourself so lightly that you do not stay on course. You are worth it! We are here to live amazing and extraordinary lives. So at this point of your life, what needs to come to an end is living a life undirected. What needs to begin is living a directed life that you create by writing down your deepest hopes.

Swimming in the Goodness is the new beginning for you. It will most certainly be a lifelong process to living out your gold. Our treasures within us are meant to be given to the world. We are designed to create and cultivate new joyful experiences, new business ventures, new friendships, and new sights for people to see. Sustain pleasant experiences, friendships, businesses, and opportunities for others. Discover your hidden passions and dreams. Bless the world by bringing forth these golden fruits. We are not meant or designed to hold onto these golden fruits within and selfishly keep them. We are designed to be bold and to live free. To be confident in knowing that our highest good is always meant to shine.

This is the new beginning of this phase of your life. Swimming in the Goodness the Golden Guide is a tool that you can always use and connect with. It has been brought forth to allow you to create a life that is amazing and extraordinary! To swim in the goodness! It is a principle and a universal law that is always sustainable. It's a principle that is applicable any day. Tap into this source, be enriched and empowered. Strengthen others by sharing this book with them. That is the beautiful process of Swimming in the Goodness, the Golden Guide. I invite you to be involved in Swimming in the Goodness Community. Be around like minded people who are passionate and thrilling. See you in the Goodness my friend!

The End

The Beginning

The only thing that liberates a person's experience is their ability of vision. Their ability to see new possibilities, to take the required action, and incur new growth.

Aaron Christopher Kirkeby

CONTACT INFORMATION

Visit Swimming in the Goodness for general information and complimentary books at

www.swimminginthegoodness.com

Send your success story or share your thoughts:

success@swimminginthegoodness.com

or

P.O. Box 880172

San Diego, Ca. 92168

Any inquiries for Speaking Engagements, Coaching Assistance, or General Info:

info@swimminginthegoodness.com

WISDOM

We are what we repeatedly do. Excellence, then, is not an act, but a habit.

Aristotle

If you can believe, all things *are* possible to him who believes.

Mark 9:23

A man with outward courage dares to die; a man with inner courage dares to live.

Lao Tzu

Success is a science; if you have the conditions, you get the result.

Oscar Wilde

Be careful what you water your dreams with. Water them with worry and fear and you will produce weeds that choke the life from your dream. Water them with optimism and solutions and you will cultivate success. Always be on the lookout for ways to turn a problem into an opportunity for success. Always be on the lookout for ways to nurture your dream.

Lao Tzu

Be as you wish to seem.

Socrates

Swimming in the Goodness

It had long since come to my attention that people of accomplishment rarely sat back and let things happen to them. They went out and happened to things.

Leonardo Da Vinci

Human behavior flows from three main sources: desire, emotion, and knowledge.

Plato

Without continual growth and progress, such words as improvement, achievement, and success have no meaning.

Benjamin Franklin

The direction in which education starts a man will determine his future in life.

Plato

We cannot always build the future for our youth, but we can build our youth for the future.

Franklin D. Roosevelt

A hero is born among a hundred, a wise man is found among a thousand, but an accomplished one might not be found even among a hundred thousand men.

Plato

All our dreams can come true, if we have the courage to pursue them.

Walt Disney

Hope is a waking dream.

Aristotle

I shall look forward to a pleasant time.

John Hancock

Every great dream begins with a dreamer. Always remember, you have within you the strength, the patience, and the passion to reach for the stars to change the world.

Harriet Tubman

Curving back within myself I create again and again.

The Bhagavad Gita

Ask and it will be given to you; seek and you will find; knock and the door will be opened to you. For everyone who asks receives; the one who seeks finds; and to the one who knocks, the door will be opened.

Mathew 7: 7-8

The future belongs to those who believe in the beauty of their dreams.

Eleanor Roosevelt

Made in the USA
San Bernardino, CA
04 October 2017